Cat and Dog

Written by Margaret Mooney
Illustrated by Meredith Thomas

sundance

A long time ago, Cat and Dog were good friends. They lived in a cave in the forest.

They spent their days together, often swimming in a water hole near the cave.

One day, as they were shaking
themselves dry after swimming,
Dog looked at Cat and burst out
laughing.

"Why are you laughing?"
asked Cat.

Dog said, "We look so shaggy.
We shake ourselves dry,
but we never comb
ourselves."

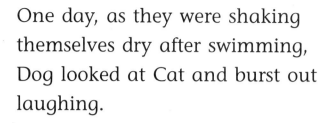

Cat was a vain creature and agreed
that they should comb each other.
Cat was also very selfish and demanded
to be combed first.

Dog began to comb Cat, using some
bamboo. He combed Cat from the top
of his ears to the tip of his tail.

Soon Cat's fur was smooth and shiny.

"Now look at your reflection in the water," said Dog.

Cat was so delighted with what he saw that he admired himself for a very long time. Dog began to get impatient.

"Hurry up! It's your turn to comb me!"

For a long time, Cat pretended not to hear. He did not want Dog to look better than he did. So Cat lingered as long as he could, gazing at his reflection.

Finally, Cat picked up the comb.
But instead of combing Dog from head
to tail, he combed him roughly from
tail to head.

Poor Dog! The rough combing hurt him. He jumped up and ran to the water to look at his reflection. He looked ridiculous.

Dog saw his hair standing up.
He knew that Cat had combed him
the wrong way on purpose.

Cat just laughed and laughed.

"I will stop your laughing!"
Dog barked. "And I will stop
being your friend!"

He was very angry, and he began
to chase Cat.

Cat kept laughing. Then he realized that Dog was about to catch him, and he quickly climbed up a tree.

Of course, Dog could not climb the tree, so he stood at the bottom and barked.

"I didn't catch you this time. But every time I see you, I will chase you and try to get you."

And from that day on, dogs have chased cats, and cats have climbed up trees to get away from dogs.